The Outlier's Choice

PRAISE FOR *THE OUTLIER'S CHOICE*

For those of us who have put our faith in Jesus Christ, the choice to be an outlier has been made. No turning back! For those outliers who have watched a child taken from you too soon, Becky's story will resonate. The pain and grief are overwhelming, no matter the age of the child or the circumstance surrounding the death. Then there are countless women who have been betrayed by their spouses' infidelity who experience unbelievable grief and pain. Cortney's story will resonate with you. What these two women did with their pain brought honor to the God of the outliers. He understands pain and grief and pulls us tightly to Himself for comfort and direction. You will think of these two women's stories long after you put the book down. Maybe, just maybe, they will light your path when you experience the darkness.

—**Sally Meredith,** teacher, author, speaker,
co-author of *Two Becoming One*, and author of
Overcoming Woundedness and *Ruth, The Story is in the Names*

Trusting God is always a choice for a Jesus follower, especially in situations which seem overwhelming. Whether or not God puts you in a situation, is he there when your world seems to be caving in? When you feel as though you can't breathe? Can you trust him to lead and strengthen you as you struggle to move forward? In *The Outlier's Choice*, Becky Huber and Cortney Donelson grapple with this issue in clear, personal, and poignant terms. No question your faith will be stimulated as you read this book!

—**Dr. Bill Ritchie,** founding pastor
of Crossroads Community Church,
author, and transformational leader

The Outlier's Choice is chock-full of wisdom nuggets that will encourage you to find purpose beyond your pain. I was immediately captivated and could not put it down. Thank you, Becky and Cortney, for your bold transparency that will empower thousands to choose an eternal focus while here on earth.

—**Christy Neal,** author of *Don't Ever Tell*
and podcast host of *Everyone Has a Voice*

Story is a powerful motivator. It gives you courage to move down paths that may be very uncomfortable. For the follower of Jesus, that difficult path of obedience to our Lord is often one that is both uncomfortable and frightening. Yet stories—Jesus's story, others' stories—give us the courage we need to stay the path. Becky and Cortney give us the courage we need through their raw and courageous stories of choosing to be obedient to God. Their stories offer hope to anyone that is wondering how the adversity in their life could really be in God's plan. They remind us that God's faithfulness is far more trustworthy than our comfort while giving practical counsel for choices that enable an eternal perspective on a daily basis.

—**Mitch White,** executive pastor at Lake Forest Church
in Huntersville, North Carolina

Cortney's and Becky's stories in *The Outlier's Choice* reassure us that in our difficult times, choosing God's way, even if not the most popular path, is worth it. God will always be with us, and we will see "His majesty unfold."

—**Stephanie Fast,** global orphan advocate and author of
She Is Mine: A War Orphan's Incredible Journey Of Survival

The Outliers Choice is about choosing to love, live, and forgive when all you really want to do is crawl up in a ball and hide from the world. In this quick and engaging book, Cortney and Becky share hard-earned wisdom gleaned from devastating loss and heartbreak that would paralyze most of us and cause us to doubt God's goodness, but instead, these circumstances drew them closer to God. Reading *The Outlier's Choice* challenged me to look at how disciples (including myself) can faithfully follow Jesus through the darkest of times.

—**Penny Noyes,** Bible teacher and author of
Seeing Value: A Biblical Perspective on Intrinsic Value
and *Responding To God: Learning from the Life
and Legacy of Hezekiah*

BECKY HUBER
CORTNEY DONELSON

THE
OUTLIER'S
CHOICE

why living an uncomfortable
life is worth it

FOREWORD BY SHEILA MANGUM

NASHVILLE

NEW YORK • LONDON • MELBOURNE • VANCOUVER

The Outlier's Choice

Why Living an Uncomfortable Life is Worth It

Published in New York, New York, by Morgan James Publishing. Morgan James is a trademark of Morgan James, LLC. www.MorganJamesPublishing.com

Proudly distributed by Ingram Publisher Services.

Morgan James BOGO™

A **FREE** ebook edition is available for you or a friend with the purchase of this print book.

CLEARLY SIGN YOUR NAME ABOVE

Instructions to claim your free ebook edition:
1. Visit MorganJamesBOGO.com
2. Sign your name CLEARLY in the space above
3. Complete the form and submit a photo of this entire page
4. You or your friend can download the ebook to your preferred device

ISBN 9781631957727 paperback
ISBN 9781631957734 ebook
Library of Congress Control Number:
2021947555

Cover Design by:
Chris Treccani
www.3dogcreative.net
Hannah Linder
http://www.hannahlinderdesigns.com

Interior Design by:
Christopher Kirk
www.GFSstudio.com

Morgan James is a proud partner of Habitat for Humanity Peninsula and Greater Williamsburg. Partners in building since 2006.

Get involved today! Visit MorganJamesPublishing.com/giving-back

To our Savior, Jesus Christ,
the girl with the big, brown eyes,
and a couple of supportive husbands.

CONTENTS

ACKNOWLEDGMENTS

From Becky

Most importantly, I thank God for meeting me on a church pew so many years ago and never leaving me to figure out life on my own.

Thank you to Shad for always telling me I can do things when I am convinced I cannot. You are my partner in life and my most favorite person.

To my kids, Josh, Hannah, and Bethany, thank you for your willingness to love your little sister even though it was risky. I am so proud of you!

To the girl with the big, brown eyes, my Rebeka Raya, thank you for letting me be your mom. I am honored to carry on your legacy through the telling of your story. I miss your raspy voice and adventurous spirit.

Cortney, I can't even believe we wrote a book together! Thank you for being my writing mentor and encouraging me. God's plan for our friendship—and this book—was set in motion years ago when we first met online. You are a kindred spirit and a dear friend to me.

Finally, I am grateful to our beta readers who took the time to read through this book and give us encouraging and constructive feedback. Thank you!

From Cortney

Sometimes, the acknowledgments are the most difficult to write. Other times, gratitude comes easy and the words flow with an appreciation that has been building in my soul for a long time. In this case, it's the latter.

First, I thank God for pulling me from certain death with a love and grace I cannot fathom nor reciprocate.

Thank you, Marc, for continuing to show everyone that our biggest and darkest secrets are the ones God uses to change the world, one individual and one marriage at a time—as long as we don't keep those secrets hidden. You are the bravest person I know. I love you.

I also thank Becky, my co-author, for agreeing to leave the safe shores of devotionals and blog posts and swim out into the ocean with me to draft this book and fine-tune it during a "meet-in-the-middle" trip to Texas. Even though we had only met in-person once before this book was written, we had been friends via email and phone calls for years—our spirits woven together through the Lord's doing, no doubt. Becky, you are like a sister to me.

To our beta readers, you are all amazing: Penny Noyes, Carol Stratton, Sue Wilson, and Kimberly Clement. And to the others in Friends with Pens: When I joined a writer's group, my introverted self believed my *I-said-yes!*-self was nuts, but my temporary insanity has resulted in many meaningful friendships and mentorships. Sheila Mangum, I'm referring to you too. I will never be able to string together the words required to describe my humble gratitude.

Together, we'd like to thank Morgan James Publishing for representing this *little book with the big message* and Sarah Greene, our proofreader. Even editors need proofreaders!

FOREWORD

The world is waiting for outliers. More specifically: God's outliers. These outliers are just *different*. They stand out (way out). *How?* Their holy choices. Their choices are against the norm, more than hard, and they need to be wrapped (smothered) with the grace and faithfulness of God to see them through.

Becky and Cortney are God's outliers. And you will want to grab your outlier's cape after reading their stories of holy choices. One called to love a young, very sick orphan long enough to show her the love of a parent until the Father could show her for Himself. One to stay and put the heartbeat back into her marriage while her own heart was shattered into un-grabbable pieces on the cold floor of deception and addiction.

Here is what you need to know. Outliers' holy choices eternally matter, as they are the actual (on Earth) love and heart of God to others (for and from Him). And, outliers are trusted to never withdraw His love or forgiveness from those in an unfinished or impossible story.

Climbing out of piles of tissues, against all statistical odds, and through the pain, outliers are the Gospel of Jesus Christ to others. How do they make such choices you ask? They know God. They follow Him. Their hearts were touched/formed when they said *yes* to the hard yet holy things.

The pure at heart see God. Becky and Cortney, show us what you have seen.

—**Sheila Mangum,** author of *The Secret of the Wedding Garment in Revelation 19:8* and former Director of Ministry Relations at Proverbs 31 Ministries

OPENING REMARKS

Becky

Cortney's husband confessed to multiple affairs and then an addiction. My daughter died of leukemia. Awash in our grief, we would have been justified in a life of anger, bitterness, and sorrow, having gone through what most would call a woman's worst nightmare.

But that was not God's plan for us. Cortney did not leave her husband. I did not fall into a pit of despair. We chose to take the life experiences we never wanted and allow God to lead us through to the other side. By taking the hand of our Heavenly Father for love, comfort, and direction, Cortney and I learned how to grow through our pain. This is the story of how we deviated from what was expected and grew closer to God as we navigated the most excruciating times of our lives.

Our stories may not be the same or even carry similar endings as yours. But the following personal accounts and practical implications will encourage you to live a godly life, no matter where God's call plants you. We hope you'll utilize the reflection and question sections, whether alone while you journal or with a group.

Our prayer is that this book—written as an afterword to Cortney's memoir, *Clay Jar Cracked: When We're Broken But Not Shattered*, and a foreword for my upcoming memoir that details my adoption journey to bring a daughter with cancer home before she went to our heavenly home—will inspire you to fully seek God in all you do so that you, too, will deviate from what is expected of culture, friends, family, and even yourself. That you will be set apart as you choose God's good purpose for your life.

ONE
SET APART

Cortney

W e spend so much time trying to fit in that, sometimes, we fail to understand that God calls us to stand out. Not in a "look at me, I'm famous" kind of way but in a way that makes others pause and ask, "What is it that makes her different?" or "How did they do that?"

These are important questions. They open the door to answers that can lead others down the path to knowing Jesus. And there is nothing more important than knowing Jesus.

> *Nevertheless,* **each person should live as a believer in whatever situation the Lord has assigned to them,** *just as God has called them* (1 Corinthians 7:17, emphasis ours).

What does it mean to live as a believer? We propose that living as a Christian believer means making choices that set us apart. Believers walk courageously—particularly if the path veers away from popular opinion—and stand with God's Word, even when it's difficult. In essence, Christians are called to live as outliers.

Ask any mathematician or scientist, and they'll tell you outliers are always real data. They dramatically affect the results. Most researchers would say outliers are legitimate observations; and, sometimes, they become the most interesting ones. They can't be ignored because what makes these data points *atypical* could make all the difference in the world. Therefore, research students are taught to investigate the nature of outliers before deciding whether or not to drop these "wayward" data points.

For the purpose of this book, an outlier is a Christian believer who is walking out that Scripture above—*accepting whatever sit-*

uation the Lord has assigned to them. It's someone who, despite what everyone else says or does, is completely sold out for God's glory, and their choices demonstrate this commitment. On the graph of life, a Christian outlier is the data point that sits away from the cluster (i.e., the "comfortable" Christians, the lukewarm Christians, the believer who follows popular opinion, or the believer who aligns with cultural expectations) . . . and does so for the glory of God.

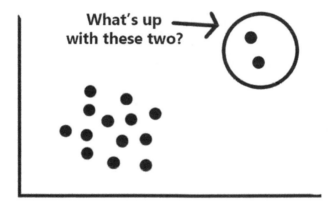

Whether outliers are categorized as bold or crazy is a matter of perspective. Either way, outliers set aside comfort—and sometimes logic—to live out God's plans, no matter the personal cost.

Jesus's disciples were outliers. They gave up everything from jobs to families—and eventually their lives—as they lived out the assignments God had given them. When you think about the disciples, when you read about their lives and their choices, what comes to mind? Do you ever put yourself in their shoes? Do you think they were bold? Crazy? Or both? Maybe you wish you had their depth of faith. Do you hope God uses you in such visible, profound, and eternal ways?

Take the Apostle Peter as an example. Early in his ministry, Peter preached only to other Jews—customary for the times and culture—but God gave him the vision of a huge sheet, one containing all types of animals, warning him not to call anything made by God impure. The message to Peter was clear: He was to include people outside of the Jewish faith in his discipleship journey. Peter obeyed God's call then baptized the Roman centurion Cornelius and his household. Peter was an outlier. He understood that the gospel was for all people, no matter how clustered they were or how seemingly far from God they lived— *even if they were gentiles, pariahs to the early Jews.* He understood God's call and obeyed it, despite it not making much sense to those around him, including the other disciples.

Make no mistake. God has a call for you too. It's a call to live as an outlier in some way. He has given you everything you need to stand out (His Word, the Holy Spirit, and the gifts of the Spirit, for example)—to be a warrior for His cause. We know: sometimes, it's difficult to discern His purposes. In some cases, you've perhaps heard God's call but chose to ignore it, running from it and assuming you couldn't do it, or more accurately (and honestly), maybe it's something you just didn't *want* to do. His request lay too far outside what would be safe or expected.

Becky and I know full well how God tends to position choices within our journeys that don't make sense. They are tugs on our hearts that go against our "better judgment." Our stories in *The Outlier's Choice* reveal this truth: We're all capable of stepping into God's call, no matter how illogical or uncomfortable it may be. Just as we're all capable of falling away from God, choosing poorly, and living out our sinful desires, each of us is also equipped to be an outlier, able to live an uncomfortable life and fully realizing that it's worth it.

All it takes are a couple of key choices. Are you ready?

Reflections & Questions
ONE

Who stands out to you in your circle of friends and family as a Christian outlier? Who is it that follows God's call, no matter the cost? Once you have them pictured firmly in your mind, list the fruits of the spirit they regularly possess or demonstrate [Love, joy, peace, forbearance, kindness, goodness, faithfulness, gentleness, and self-control" (Galatians 5:22–23)]. Which one seems paramount to their mission and why? Which one(s) do you feel you lack in your current season of life? Ask God to provide.

If you are currently planted in the cluster, living a comfortable life among your Christian friends, how do you feel about the content of this book (especially this first chapter)? Are you nervous? Excited? Apathetic? Explain.

TWO
THE GREATEST EXAMPLE

Becky

A s followers of Jesus, God has a calling on each of our lives. In John 3:30, John the Baptist sums up that calling: "He must become greater; I must become less." We are called to respond to life in the same way John the Baptist did. We are called to become more like Jesus. To understand how to become more like Jesus, let's take a look at his life first.

The greatest outlier of all time was Jesus Christ. He stood out from the pack everywhere he went. His life began when he was born in a barn to a virgin. From day one, Jesus already stood out. So much so, shepherds and wisemen came from far away to see him. At twelve years old, his parents found him in the temple "sitting among the teachers, listening to them and asking them questions. Everyone who heard him was amazed at his understanding and his answers" (Luke 2:46b–47). As an adult, much to the dismay of the religious leaders, Jesus would be found in the company of tax collectors, misfits, lepers, and sinners. He did not follow the customs and expectations of a traditional Jewish man; he followed his calling from God: "to save the world through him" (John 3:17b).

Jesus explained to his disciples that he "must go to Jerusalem and suffer many things at the hands of the elders, chief priests, and teachers of the law and that he must be killed and on the third day be raised to life" (Matthew 16:21). Jesus knew going to Jerusalem would lead to great suffering and death, and he still went. He chose to follow God's plan for his life because he knew the outcome would be greater than the pain he was about to endure. When he was arrested, he didn't resist. When they questioned him, he didn't defend himself or argue. When they tortured him, he didn't fight back. When he hung on the cross, he didn't curse them. In fact, he asked God to forgive them. And when he knew he would die, he simply said, "It is finished" and relinquished his spirit.

Jesus is the greatest example of an outlier because he never worried about what the people around him thought about his mission. He didn't question God or try to run from Him. He simply lived the life God was asking him to live.

For six hours Jesus hung on the cross. Every moment, it became more and more difficult to breathe. The pain he endured was excruciating. Imagine being there, at the foot of the cross, watching the one you love struggle to take even one ragged breath. Imagine the devastation and the heavy weight of grief overcome you as his head slumps over, never to be lifted again. Now, picture the sky growing dark in the middle of the day, matching the darkness in your heart. Feel the ground beginning to shake and rocks splitting open. Listen as the sound of the moving earth matches the wail of your sorrow. Jesus, the man you have been following for three years is dead. All must be lost, right?

> *The earth shook and the rocks split. When the centurion and those with him who were guarding Jesus saw the earthquake and all that had happened, they were terrified, and exclaimed, "Surely he was the Son of God!"* (Matthew 27:51 and 54).

When the centurion and the men guarding Jesus witnessed his death, they became fully aware that he was who he said he was. Like a slap to the face, they were hit with the realization that Jesus was, indeed, the Son of God. And it scared them. They felt the magnitude of what they had done: crucified the Son of God. In Jesus's death, the ones killing him could see he was their Savior. Isn't it amazing to see that God can use the darkest moment, the most hopeless situation, for His glory?

If we want to become more like Jesus, our lives must mimic his life. We must follow God, even if it separates us from the rest of humanity. We must choose the things He is calling us to, just like Jesus did. That may mean choosing to go after things that are out of the ordinary or make us look strange. When we do, God will use us to show others Himself.

Thankfully, for all humanity, this was not the end of the story. We must remember that Jesus said in Matthew 6:21, he "must be killed," but he also said, "on the third day be raised to life." On the third day, he did rise from the dead. When Mary Magdalene and the other Mary went to his tomb, they found the stone rolled away and an angel sitting on it (Matthew 28:1–4). He told them, "Do not be afraid, for I know that you are looking for Jesus, who was crucified. He is not here; he has risen, just as he said" (Matthew 28:5). Jesus is alive!

The greatest gift of God is the life, death, and resurrection of His son. "For God so loved the world that he gave his one and only Son, that whoever believes in him shall not perish but have eternal life" (John 3:16). We all have the option of eternal life—all we need to do is believe. That is what makes us followers of God. When we believe, we receive the salvation of God. He sanctifies us and makes us holy, like Jesus. As we grow in our holiness, our lives mimic the life of Jesus. As our lives become more like Jesus, we can choose to become outliers for Christ.

Reflections & Questions
TWO

What does it mean to allow for Jesus to become more and for you to become less (John 3:30)? *How* (specifically) are you allowing Jesus to become more in your life? *How* are you allowing yourself to become less? Are you following the customs of the world or the calling of God on your life?

Have you ever really considered what Jesus went through physically and emotionally on the day he died for you? Has it "hit you" the way it did the centurion that Jesus is the Son of God? Take a moment to write or speak aloud in your group a prayer of thanksgiving for Jesus's suffering for your salvation.

Are you aware of God's calling on your life? Have you prayed and asked Him to reveal it to you? Have you been aware of it for years but been afraid to pursue it? Does it feel too scary or too big?

Have you received the gift of eternal life that God is offering you? Have you received His forgiveness for your sins? Do you know there is nothing too big He can't forgive? We encourage you to stop now and pray this prayer:

Dear God, I know I am a sinner. Please forgive me of my sins. I believe in your life, death, and resurrection on the cross. I receive your gift of forgiveness and eternal life right now. Please come into my life and teach me how to follow you. In Jesus's name, amen.

THREE
FIERY FURNACE

Becky

I exited the airplane bearing the weight of our newly adopted daughter's emaciated body strapped to my chest. In a dreamy trance of disbelief, I held fast to my husband, Shad's, hand and let him lead me through the airport concourse. Our sleep-deprived bodies had just traveled across the globe from Bulgaria to Portland, Oregon: a trip that takes over a day to complete. The excitement of our arrival trumped the weariness of our bones from the long trip.

"I can't believe we're actually doing this! We are home with our daughter!" I said.

"This is crazy," Shad agreed.

We made our way down the long, deserted corridor to the airport lobby. The clock on the wall read ten thirty p.m. The automatic doors scraped open; we stepped through the threshold and were greeted by the joyous cheers of our family and closest friends.

"Welcome home!" and "They're finally here!" filled our ears and our hearts. The airport party I had been imagining for four years was finally a reality. Rebeka hung quietly in the front pack amid all the excitement, unaware of her celebrity status. Her curious eyes darted around from one elated stranger's face to the other. She had no idea this was all for her. Everyone was here to catch a glimpse of the little girl from Bulgaria. The girl with the big, brown eyes and the body full of cancer.

The first time I stared into those eyes was in a picture sent from our adoption agency. In the email titled "Special Treasure," they described Rebeka as "a beautiful two-year-old girl who has been longing for a family to love and adore her!" I couldn't imagine why she was two years old and still didn't have a forever family. The next sentence ended my wondering: "After medical assessments, they found out she has leukemia but is in remission." The words on the screen began to blur. It took a moment for me to realize they were blurred because my phone was shaking in my trembling hands. Something about her grabbed my attention. Yet my gut reaction was to close the email, turn off my phone, and put it away.

We weren't planning to adopt a sick child, but as hard as I tried to ignore the email, I felt a nudge. I knew the nudge. It was gentle yet firm. It was the same nudge I had felt four years before when God first spoke to my heart about adoption. I retrieved my phone out of my purse and reopened the Special Treasure email.

I learned later that day that Shad had been looking at the same email and had felt the same gentle nudge. Before the sun set on that warm June afternoon, we left a message for our case worker to tell us more about this girl named Rebeka.

Through the power of that holy prompting from God, I listened to our case worker describe Rebeka as a fierce princess, a fighter. The cancer—leukemia—was in remission, but Rebeka still required a bone marrow transplant for a chance at a full recovery. She just needed a family willing to give her that chance. We contacted an international adoption doctor to look over Rebeka's medical information and give us her professional opinion about her health and development. Shad and I sat in our living room with the doctor on speaker phone and listened as she told us just how rare and serious Rebeka's leukemia was. We hung up the phone discouraged. We both knew God was asking us to consider being her forever family, but logic screamed that this was too risky.

Our discussions were chock-full of questions and prayers:

Why would God show us this little girl if He wasn't asking us to adopt her?

Why would God ask us to adopt a sick child?

How can we do this to ourselves and our family?

How can we go to Bulgaria, rip this child out of the only life she has ever known, only to bring her here to poke and prod?

Through prayer, we determined the only answer was to obey God. He had placed her in our line of vision, and He was asking us to go after her. So we said yes. With the stroke of the keyboard, I filled out an application that asked the Bulgarian government to allow us to adopt Rebeka. Just a few weeks later, we received the good news that the Bulgarian officials had agreed. While we fought to expedite the adoption process, Rebeka lay in Bulgaria fighting against the deadly beast that was trying to overtake her tiny body.

We arrived home just in time to find out the leukemia she had been battling since she was eight months old had advanced to crisis mode. We would soon realize that getting her home safely would be the easy part. The real fight was about to begin. What was once a slow-moving disease was now full-blown. She had no muscle tone in her body and was too weak to sit up on her own. At two years and eight months, she weighed a mere seventeen pounds: the weight of a tiny one-year-old.

For the first time in her life, Rebeka wasn't fighting leukemia alone. She had a mom and dad by her side, advocating for her and loving her. And she grew to love us. We bonded as a family of six: Shad, Josh, Hannah, Bethany, Rebeka, and me.

Rebeka nestled into our laps day after day and we rocked. We handed her bottles full of sustenance, and she slapped our hand away. No one had taught her the polite way to say she wanted to hold things herself. We wore a rut in the hallway, pushing an IV pole while simultaneously pulling Rebeka in the wagon. I sang the ABCs to her in the middle of a CT scan while wearing a seven-pound lead apron to protect me from the x-rays being emitted into her body. Rebeka demanded that I stand next to her bed and hold her hand while she slept, and my head bobbed up and down from sheer exhaustion.

Finally, after three months of toxic chemotherapy, we received the bone marrow biopsy results: fifty percent leukemia cells. We had prayed for five percent. That one zero changed the course of her treatment and her life. She would not qualify for a bone marrow transplant, her only chance at a long-term remission. They could not save her. The words filled our ears and ripped open our hearts.

I gasped for breath as the grief of the devastating news weighed me down, as if I was wearing ten lead aprons. My pile of soggy napkins grew taller and taller as Shad and I discussed our options. The only answer was the worst answer. We took her home the next day. Rebeka needed to know being in a hospital or institution was not normal kid-life.

As her body filled with leukemia cells, she thrived. She played. She rode a tricycle. She went to the beach. She went for walks. She slept on the floor. She watched movies. She danced to loud music. She nibbled on food and was nourished by tube feedings. She felt good on some days and horrible on other days.

We prayed for a healing miracle. We knew God had a plan for her life, even if her life was much shorter than we wanted it to be. We lived each day loving Rebeka with our eyes always puffy. We slept little, cried often, and played a lot. We looked to God to fill our hearts with joy and hope even as we anticipated the deep grief we sensed was on the horizon.

"How do we do this?" Shad asked me three weeks after we left the hospital. We sat together on the couch. Josh, Hannah, and Bethany were in their beds upstairs. Rebeka snored softly on the floor at our feet.

"What do you mean?" I asked.

"The oral medications don't seem to be slowing down the leukemia. We keep praying for God to heal her. What if He doesn't?" he asked through a thick throat.

"I know. I've been thinking about that too." I paused, not wanting to say the next sentences that God had lain on my heart. "I think God is asking us to start praying a different prayer. The same prayer Shadrach, Meshach, and Abednego prayed before they were thrown into the fiery furnace. They knew He could save them, but they said they would praise Him even if He didn't."

Only the whir of Rebeka's feeding pump could be heard as we thought on that conundrum. He may not heal her, but we'll still praise Him? By human standards, it made no sense. But the Holy Spirit in us said it was the only thing that *did* make sense. It was at this moment something shifted. Our perspective changed. The only way we would survive the blazing heat of our fiery furnace was to step in.

"I think you're right. . . . That's all we can do now. God is our only hope," Shad said after careful consideration.

"Okay. Let's pray now," I answered as I took his hands in mine. "God, we know you can heal Rebeka, right here, right now. We know it only takes a word for you to heal her. But, if you don't heal her here on earth, and you take her home to Heaven, we will still worship you. We will still love and trust you. Please continue to comfort our hearts as we walk this journey with Rebeka. Amen."

Only a week later, in her home, surrounded by her dad, mom, brother, and two sisters, Rebeka Raya breathed her last breath. With a tiny puff of air, her soul joined Jesus in Heaven while her body was nestled in her big sister's arms. It was a Thursday, only one month after they told us she would not survive. Four months after she arrived in America. And just three weeks shy of her third birthday.

Reflections & Questions
THREE

Have you ever prayed for a miracle? Did God give you what you asked for? Or did He answer your prayer in a different way?

Have you ever had to face a fiery furnace in your life (Daniel 3)? Did you choose to worship God in the flames? If so, how did worshipping God affect your outlook on the situation? Or did the furnace turn you away from God? If so, how has that affected the trajectory of your life?

Have you experienced grief in your life? Have you allowed God to comfort you? Do you think it is possible to experience joy in the midst of grief? Explain.

FOUR
THREE HOLY WORDS

Cortney

On a warm, late-summer evening, while the kids lay dreaming in the safety of their rooms, I bounded up the stairs to distance myself from the man I had stood in front of the altar with more than a decade before.

My internal dialogue wouldn't quit.

You deserve better.

You have to leave.

This isn't worth fighting for.

I wouldn't even let myself ask *that big* question: "What did I do wrong?"

I knew there was no good answer for that one—no use in wasting my time or heartache. I wasn't usually one to take responsibility for others' actions. I knew full well there was nothing I could have done differently.

My husband, Marc, had just admitted to being unfaithful. Not once. And not twice. He had, over the past three days, revealed multiple affairs that spanned our entire marriage, the by-product of a fifteen-year secret addition to pornography, which had started with a glance toward someone else's computer screen in our college's Communications and Technology department.

Without any red flags, I had been blindsided.

We all know the genesis of an addiction doesn't lie with the vice. But access to this particular addiction literally sits in the palms of our hands. It's more common than I ever knew—but would soon learn, having now been forced to experience the catastrophic consequences.

On "day one" of this crisis, I found myself face-down on a pillow, screaming at the top of my lungs. My only goal? To release the pain. Emotional pain is just as tactile as physical pain. My husband's initial revelation left me fractured. I couldn't see the room around me. I couldn't hear any of the words Marc said after those first and most damaging ones, his confession:

We had sex.

I could only feel.

I remember the feel of that pillow, the pounding of my heart, the warmth of my cheeks, the tremor in my hands . . . even the give of the padded carpet beneath my toes on the stairs as I bounded up them thirty minutes later, searching for Marc after handing our toddler to a neighbor to watch for a few hours.

Two days later, after more revelations from my husband, my heightened sense of touch—of feel—morphed into an ability to hear clearly. That evening, through my tornado of emotions, my internal voice sounded loud and confused, even hysterical.

Just grab the kids and leave him!

I sat atop the comforter on our bed, not finding any comfort at all. I pulled my Bible off of the nightstand and opened it haphazardly. In my head, I had given up, but my heart didn't want to follow. Logic pried its way through my feelings, covering me with the sad knowledge that most marriages don't survive this kind of trauma. But memories of our dating years, our early marriage, and, yes, from just the month before—along with my love for our cozy family of four—begged me to avoid admitting that our thirteen-year marriage was likely over. I straddled a precarious abyss, the majority of my mind and body on the side that would thrust me into the darkness named "divorce."

"God, what do I do with this?" I spoke my plea out loud. Then I squeezed my eyes shut and wept.

"Don't leave yet."

I snapped my eyes open, and the hot tears on my cheeks seemed to evaporate instantly. I couldn't have known it then, but those words would alter the course of my life.

The words *don't leave yet* were spoken with gentle authority. Later, I'd say they were "self-authenticating." The voice of God was calm, purposed, and filled with love—the opposite of my frantic inner thoughts.

God didn't make a demand. He didn't throw Scripture at me, pointing me to a specific verse in the Bible that lay on my lap. Instead, those three words spoke volumes about His character and held the answer I had been seeking for what to do.

Every word counted, especially the word *yet*. Three tiny words to parallel Marc's three-word admission that had left me undone on the living room floor. While providing a plan, God simultaneously offered me an exit strategy, one I could choose at any moment. The word *yet* was the most loving word of all and became an anchor for my soul. God had given me a sense of freedom, even though I still felt trapped by my husband's disclosures. It was a freedom born from having choices.

It only took a moment for me to trust that voice. It belonged to God, whom I knew to be sovereign and good. I slipped off the bed, descended the stairs, and sat down next to Marc to start the long, hard work of recovery and forgiveness. On that couch—the one that held the cream-colored pillow I had screamed into only two days before—I looked straight ahead, unable to make eye contact, and whispered, "You may have broken your vows, but I don't have to break mine." It became a pivotal moment in our relationship.

It would take years, but the journey toward redemption—for both of us—began that night. With each passing month, there was healing.

People often ask me why I didn't leave my husband. It's a valid question with a difficult answer. I'm fearful it requires a certain measure of faith and an intimate relationship with our Heavenly Father on the part of the questioner to fully understand my perspective—my choice.

Each day during those first few weeks, I asked God to release me from the pain, from the marriage itself. I was met with the memory of God's voice on "day three." *Don't leave yet.* So, I bent my knees in prayer and fought for the marriage for another day.

My choices to stay and wrestle through this story, build back a marriage that had been desecrated, and manage my anger toward countless people stood in stark contrast to the way I was raised, which was to be strong and independent—to look out for myself. I firmly believed that I deserved *better*. My choice to stay and battle heartache, betrayal, and the spiritual forces hellbent on tearing our marriage apart defied my own logic. It just didn't make sense. Yet, I continued to ignore my common sense, the statistical norms surrounding addiction and infidelity, and our cultural and societal beliefs.

I shared my struggle with only half a handful of people, understanding the judgment that would come from many people might affect my ability to hear God's will and guidance. I knew I would have been part of that judging majority had this happened to someone I knew. My own advice was to leave!

Little did I know at the time, but by holding this story close, keeping it mostly private, listening only to God's voice through all the emotional chaos, and pushing down the lies that rose up, I was well on my way to becoming an outlier.

I stayed that night (and every night thereafter) *because God asked me to trust Him*, not just with the situation at hand but with my children's security, my husband's soul, and my bleeding heart.

I leaned into hope, which can often be a tricky dance. Hope is not the same as expectation, as so many—myself included at one point—assume. When hope morphs into expectation, we find ourselves disappointed with outcomes, betrayed by loved ones, and crushed by unmet dreams. The hope I found had a name . . .

I didn't expect God to heal my marriage or "fix" my spouse. I put my hope into believing that His promises are true. I put my hope in the assurance that my definition of *good* wasn't *good enough* and God would supernaturally work all things the way He promises—for the *(ultimate)* good of those who love Him (Romans 8:28). Even if that means divorce. Pain. Sorrow. No matter the outcome, I chose to put my hope in God, believing that I would be okay because His will would be done.

> *I trusted that the Lord who chose me was fully able to lead me into and through this crisis, growing me into the woman He had appointed me to be . . . while also working to restore the man He created my spouse to be.*

I searched for every ounce of respect, truth, and trust that had been stolen between Marc and me, gathered it back up, and directed it toward God instead. I put all of *my* trust into what I had learned and experienced of His faithfulness in the past in the hope that I'd find a better tomorrow.

The Lord is my strength and my shield; in him my heart
trusts, and I am helped; my heart exults, and with my
song I give thanks to him (Psalm 28:7).

I imagine mine was a similar choice to the one that Jesus's disciples had to make when Jesus invited them to "Follow me" back in 30 A.D. The Bible portrays these poignant invitations as if the requests were followed by consistently quick answers in the affirmative. Just as I seemed to easily slide off my bed and obey God's request to stay in my marriage that night, the disciples purportedly dropped their jobs and left their boats, tables, and families with ease. Why?

God had called us, and we understood that the
best choice was to become Christian outliers.

In all of these cases, we see the mark of the time-tested choice of *God over self*. It's the choice of James and John, brothers called away from their father and their nets to become fishers of men. Later, James would choose God over self again when he was the first disciple martyred for his faith.

It's the choice Adam and Eve had when they risked reaching into that tree in the Garden. In their case, they seemingly chose *self over God* as they took bites of the forbidden fruit.

In my life, I have been no wiser, no less doubtful of God's promises than those first humans in Eden. Like the profit Jeremiah, I, too, have been duped by my deceitful heart, my pride, and Satan himself. In my past, I have felt the sting of choosing self over God and reaped the consequences of complacency, ignorance, selfishness, and fear. And I admit, there have also been times when I've responded with a flat-out "no" to God's calls or promptings.

Through all of these experiences, I have learned this: God over self is every bit the most difficult *and* the easiest decision to make. And, at least in this chapter of my life story, I chose the uncomfortable but *best* option: to trust God.

That humid, early September evening, I chose to become an outlier and set aside everything I had learned and every worldly desire and expectation I held to follow Him. That's when I left my spot on my comforter to enter the holy position of trusting God. In doing so, my surrendered heart paved the way for Him to show up in a mighty way.

And because of His goodness and faithfulness, I aim to follow Him all the days of my life.

Reflections & Questions
FOUR

Have you ever found yourself in a situation where emotional overload caused you to make a rash choice? What was the end result? Today, if you had that same opportunity, what choice would you make? Are there amends you should make or a request for forgiveness (from the Lord) to wrestle with?

Have you ever heard the voice of God in your spirit? How would you describe it? Have you heard God through the messages of others? What is one especially poignant example?

Do you understand Cortney's fear in trying to explain why she was able to trust God almost instantly, go back to her husband, and be willing to work it out? How would you explain to non-believers this choice to act so illogically?

Is there an uncomfortable choice you have to make in your life right now? What is stopping you from choosing to become an outlier? Is it fear? Shame? Doubt? Pride? Perhaps you haven't discerned God's way yet. Explain what's holding you back and list/share what steps you can take to overcome the resistance.

MAKING THE UNCOMFORTABLE CHOICE

Cortney

imagine for some of you, Becky's and my stories outline choices reserved for the deeply faithful.

While faith is required, it's a faith born from the knowledge that there is a God who loves us completely, not a level of faith we earn through years of devotion to Christ. I am not a spiritual giant. I am often weak, prideful, and full of doubt. I love how Paul described this struggle of the flesh and heart when he wrote to the Romans:

> *I do not understand what I do. For what I want to do, I do not do, but what I hate, I do* (Romans 7:15).

Perhaps you understand this struggle, too?

The truth is that anyone can choose God's will. Anyone can glorify God by setting aside themselves to become outliers for His Kingdom's causes. We're just one *daily* choice away.

Others of you may be wondering what it means to *hear God*. I can only honestly discuss this from my experiences. At times, I hear God inside my head. It's a voice—not my own—that I have learned to recognize as that of the One who holds everything in His hands. It's not frequent, but it happens when I'm willing to listen and when I believe it's possible to hear Him at all. I hear His voice when I pray in the quiet spaces of my life.

I believe God speaks differently to different people at different times, depending on our relationship with Him and how best we might hear Him. He doesn't want to be a mystery. God wants us to know Him and discern His plans. His goal is not to confuse us but to build us up and then set us loose. Some of us hear God in our spirits (much like that voice I describe);

others through spending time in His Creation—surrounded by nature—and still others through promptings that originate from conversations with godly people.

> *Whether you turn to the right or to the left, your ears will hear a voice behind you, saying, "This is the way; walk in it"* (Isaiah 30:21).

On the journey to becoming an outlier for Christ, hearing God is only half of the pilgrimage. We can hear and choose not to obey. We can hear and doubt God's words or goodness. We can hear and believe we know more about ourselves and our situations or have a better plan. Or . . . as Becky and I chose to do through our difficult circumstances, we can hear and trust.

> *Trust in the LORD with all your heart and lean not on your own understanding; in all your ways submit to him, and he will make your paths straight* (Proverbs 3:5–6).

Outliers throw caution to the wind, surrendering their ideas of what's best for God's plans of what's good. It's a weird approach, right? Throw away *best* for *good*. But it's a worthy strategy, a holy opportunity. I've learned God's *good* is way better than my *best*.

Becky trusted God with her heart and her family. And even after her heart broke with grief and loss, she continues to trust. Why? She keeps her eyes on the eternal picture, realizing God's glory is the goal—the end game. Becky knows others are watching, and the way she walks out her story will either point others to our Heavenly Father or suggest He is not worthy to follow with our whole lives. She's choosing the former.

I trusted God with my heart and my family. Why? I kept my eyes on the eternal picture. I trusted God with my marriage, even as my heart broke with betrayal because He assured me the story—and my pain—served a bigger purpose than just for me. My heartache would not be in vain. God doesn't allow suffering without purpose.

He invited me to be a part of what He was doing to preserve the sanctity of marriage and show others that grace of an epic proportion is possible. And I accepted. Since then, it's been a glorious journey.

> Jesus said to her, "Did I not tell you that if you believed you would see the glory of God?" (John 11:40, ESV).

God redeemed what my husband and I could not have fixed on our own. I learned that all-out trust should be reserved for God alone. We humans carry too much of the world with us. We're not perfect. We can't be. But God is, and it's for this reason that I trust Him completely—but not my husband. Some may think it's sad for a spouse to say this of their partner (that they can't be trusted one hundred percent) or that I'm choosing a negative mindset or sabotaging our marriage. It's okay if you believe that. As my husband and I have stumbled through our faith journeys, it's been refreshing for us to let each other off the hook of perfection. After all, it's a little too prickly and a whole lot draining for us.

> *When we traded the pedestals we had built for each other for God's throne, we never felt so free to be who He created us to be.*

That's grace.

You may not be called to adopt, love a child with a terminal illness, remain married through a similar story of betrayal, or become marriage mentors. But we can guarantee you'll be called out of the cluster to do something uncomfortable, to be stretched for His glory, to impact others in ways that make people cringe or balk. Perhaps God has called you to:

- Schedule that mission trip
- Serve the homeless in your community/provide hospitality that goes beyond the norm
- Give up that high-paying job that stresses your values or compromises family time
- Stop gossiping and encourage others to do the same
- Serve as a youth volunteer at your church
- Give above a tithe or be generous in ways that don't make sense
- Write the book/start the blog
- Foster a child
- Give up that vice/idol
- Forgive someone from your past who doesn't even know they hurt you
- Leave relationships when God releases you, even when others believe you should stay
- Continue to lean on God when challenges persist longer than expected

Being an outlier for Christ means we're set apart, but it will look differently for each of us, depending on God's great purposes, our free will, and the gifting He has entrusted to us.

Outliers understand there is a larger stage, one where we aren't the protagonists or the heroes. God is the Alpha and

Omega. The beginning and the end. There is no better story than His. We just have to choose. If we choose God's way, we may feel awkward, alone, or silly, but God is always with us. And we'll be rewarded as we watch His majesty unfold.

Reflections & Questions
FIVE

Cortney talks about how no minimum measure of faith is required for hearing God or choosing to live life for His glory. Do you ever compare your "level of faith" to others' faith journeys? How and in what ways? If so, what negative messages or lies have you believed about your own faith that you can now set aside to live in greater freedom?

Cortney mentions only trusting God one hundred percent and no one else, not even her husband of decades. What do you think about Cortney's statement about not trusting her husband completely while also saying they now have the strongest, most intimate relationship they've ever had? Is this possible? Shouldn't you trust your spouse completely?

Betrayal is one of the most damaging relational conflicts. Have you ever been betrayed by someone you trusted completely? What was the outcome? Have you forgiven that person? Is there room for forgiveness *and reconciliation*, particularly if you use the power of the Holy Spirit? How might you go about that process?

WE DON'T WALK ALONE

Becky

Whwhen we walk through circumstances that are difficult and scary, God is faithful to give us exactly what we need. He doesn't put us in a situation and leave us alone to figure it out.

He didn't ask me to adopt a little girl with leukemia and then say, "Okay, you've got this. Let me know how it goes." He didn't sit on His heavenly throne listening to Cortney's husband confess his infidelity and say to her, "Now you know. What are you going to do about it?" No, when we are standing at the edge of the unknown, He exhorts us to "Be strong and courageous. Do not be afraid or terrified because of them, for the Lord your God goes with you; he will never leave you nor forsake you" (Deuteronomy 31:6). God is right here with us, making us strong and courageous.

It is easy to listen to our guts and let our feelings dictate our actions. When I first looked into Rebeka's big, brown eyes, my hands began to tremble and my breathing quickened. The tiny girl with leukemia scared me. But I chose to let God make me brave, and I opened the email again. I stared into her eyes and considered her diagnosis. I opened the short video and watched her smile as she sat on the white swing pushing the buttons on her remote control. My heart began to open as I felt God lift my chin, look into my eyes, and ask me if I would say yes—a decision that would lead me to set aside my fear and comfort in exchange for trust in His good plan.

This was not the only time He would ask Shad and I to say yes. The road to Rebeka was paved with many yeses. At every turn and roadblock, God would ask again, "Will you trust me?" The more we learned about Rebeka, the more we had to trust Him. One doctor told us she had never seen a family go after a child that would most likely die. From her point of view, it didn't make sense for us to put ourselves through all the work and heartache of adopting Rebeka if she was most likely not going to survive. She only said what most people were thinking. But God gave us the stubborn resolve to say, "We aren't most people. We are going to adopt her." He was making us strong and courageous.

God gave us the courage to fall in love with Rebeka as we fought cancer alongside her. We could have held back until we thought it was safe to go all in. God gave us the tenderness to love the little girl with the big, brown eyes simply because she was our daughter. In the end, our hearts were ripped in two. I am very grateful for mourning because it means I got to love her. We lost our daughter, but I am thankful I can say "my daughter."

For three years, I have been making my way out of the fog of grief. My greatest comfort has been God. In Matthew 5:4, Jesus says, "Blessed are they who mourn, for they will be comforted." Blessed means happy or blissful. Is Jesus really saying a person can be happy or blissful while mourning? *Yes.*

He is saying our happiness is independent of our circumstances. Because of the Holy Spirit in us, as followers of Jesus, we can go through the unthinkable (the loss of a child or the confession of infidelity from our spouse, for example) and still feel the joy of the Lord. There have been days when I could barely emerge from beneath my covers in the morning. Days when I made it out of bed then landed in my favorite chair for the day. I have even slid to the floor in front of my chair, staring into nothing as I lay in the fetal position.

At times, grief has been heavy and has zapped my energy. But my hand always finds my Bible, opens the pages, and finds joy in the Word. God meets me in my bed, in my chair, on the floor, and in my grief and reminds me that He is my joy, peace, and strength. I can sit up, take a deep breath, and get up from the floor. The grief is still with me, but it is not pinning me down. God has shown me how to live with grief and not let it rule over me.

Anyone can choose to be an outlier for Jesus. He has a good plan for each of our lives, no matter our shortcomings or mistakes. Take Mary Magdalene for example. She joined Jesus and walked with him during his ministry. She didn't follow Jesus because she was a great and holy woman. In fact, in Luke 8:2b, it says, "Mary (called Magdalene) from whom seven demons had come out." Mary Magdalene was possessed by seven demons when she first met Jesus. After he drove them out, she could have walked away and lived in shame. She could have walked away and simply gone back to her normal life. Instead, she chose to walk with Jesus and the disciples "helping to support them out of her own means" (Luke 8:3b).

We find Mary Magdalene with Jesus, again, when he dies on the cross. "Many women were there, watching from a distance. They had followed Jesus from Galilee to care for his needs. Among them were Mary Magdalene, Mary the mother of James and Joseph, and the mother of Zebedee's sons" (Matthew 27:55–56). It had to be difficult to be by Jesus's side as he was put to death. Even his own disciple, Peter, denied knowing Jesus three times. But Mary Magdalene chose to remain an outlier for Jesus as she waited at the foot of the cross to attend to his needs.

Jesus continues to rely on Mary Magdalene's choice to be an outlier one more time. As she approached his tomb, she found the stone in front rolled away and an angel of the Lord sitting atop. He tells her that Jesus is not in the tomb but has risen and she "hurried away, afraid yet filled with joy, and ran to tell the disciples" (Matthew 28:8). Later, Jesus meets her on the path and tells her to go and tell the disciples where he will appear to them. Jesus chose to appear to her because she had shown him that she chose to say yes to the hard things to honor him. Being an outlier for Jesus means saying yes to his good plan and walking through it "afraid yet filled with joy."

Like Mary Magdalene, Cortney and I made the choice to follow God's way in the face of adversity. Instead of leaving her husband, Cortney chose to reach for her Bible, stay, and allow God to heal her relationship. Instead of falling deep into the pit of grief, I chose to reach for my Bible and allow God to show me how to find joy in the midst of grief. We chose to sit away from the cluster on the graph of life, completely sold out for the glory of God. My prayer is that you, too, will allow God to make you strong and courageous, so you can experience a life completely sold out for His glory.

Reflections & Questions
SIX

Have you ever felt like you couldn't trust God? Like He let you down? How did it make you feel? Angry? Unsettled? Afraid? Doubtful of God's goodness? Did you face the doubt and allow God to bring you through it to a deeper trust in Him? Tell someone about it.

Have you been in a difficult situation and felt like God was making you strong and courageous through it? Have you been in a difficult situation and "muscled your way through" in your own strength? What's the difference? And what was the outcome of each?

Have you ever felt God asking you to do something and told Him no? Have you felt God asking you to do something and said yes? Compare the outcomes?

SEVEN
THREE-DIMENSIONAL

Cortney

As humans living on this ball of rock and water, one of our fatal flaws is the propensity to view our lives only from the perspective of the here and now. It's easy to get caught up in worldly circumstances because our physical senses deceive us. We tend to believe that what we feel, hear, taste, touch, and see are the only things that matter—and not just matter, but are the only things that exist.

So when things go sideways, devastation hits, or loss pierces our hearts, we focus on what we can sense in our physical world. We hurl our words. Anger swells. Fists rise. Relationships break. We crave power when we feel powerless, and often, revenge seems more appropriate than forgiveness. For some, the flight side of our innate response kicks in, and we flee, escaping our struggles through avoidance or some coping mechanism that will never glorify God.

We forget there is another dimension, not only of this world but *within us*, as well.

God made us three-dimensional. We are body, soul, *and* spirit in one. First Thessalonians 5:23 confirms this:

> Now may the God of peace himself sanctify you completely, and may your whole spirit and soul and body be kept blameless at the coming of our Lord Jesus Christ (ESV).

For Christ followers, the "spirit" is the Holy Spirit; God is with us.

In God's Word, the soul dimension is also referred to as the heart. Our soul is what makes us, well . . . *us*. It encompasses everything we think, feel, and believe, leading us to our choices and actions. And our bodies—our physical dimensions? They are our "for this earth" vessels—our physical selves and all the senses that come with us.

If we only respond to our circumstances and to others with our bodies and hearts (our senses, thoughts, and feelings), we are not utilizing our full potential—namely the spiritual dimension. We aren't living with and through God's mighty power. In His power, the lame walk, the blind see, hearts are transformed, complete forgiveness is possible, and death is not the last word in our stories. If we tap into the Holy Spirit and live in alignment with our holy Perfector, anything is possible. But if we ignore the Spirit, we only satisfy our own desires, making God inconsequential in our lives. When we operate apart from God, we are limited to our own thoughts, ideas, actions of the flesh, and the physical world around us.

> But I say, walk by the Spirit, and you will not gratify the desires of the flesh. For the desires of the flesh are against the Spirit, and the desires of the Spirit are against the flesh, for these are opposed to each other, to keep you from doing the things you want to do (Galatians 5:16–17, ESV).

If we only see and experience the world in our vacuum of space and time, we miss the point of everything. We miss eternity. The truth is that our lives here are but a blip on the continuum of existence. When we think everything is about us—and about the here and now—we minimize God and His whole Creation, *including ourselves*.

Eternity with our Heavenly Father is our goal. Not happiness. Not comfort. Not success. Not even physical life. When we choose eternity over our current circumstances—when we choose God over ourselves—and when we become outliers for Christ, we remind the world that our current reality is not our permanent reality.

When I slipped off that bed and trusted God to help my husband and me work through our crisis, I had to set aside my heart (my hurt, the anger, any doubts, and my negative thoughts) and choose to listen to my spirit (the Holy Spirit because I've put my faith in Jesus). I had to choose the most difficult path at that moment and trust that God's plan, made known to me in my spirit, was the right path. The eternal plan. The *best choice*.

Outliers embrace this eternal mindset and, ideally, influence those around them to do the same. There is an inexplicable joy and peace found in the life of a Christian outlier. That joy and peace attract others, often motivating them to ask, "How do you do it?" or "Why would you do that?"

Why would you adopt a child with cancer from across the globe? [That's crazy.]

How did you forgive your husband? [I couldn't have done that.]

Why would you put your family through that? [It doesn't seem worth it.]

How did your marriage survive? [Most don't/Mine wouldn't.]

These types of questions [and the thoughts attached to them] open the door to conversations about Jesus. That's crucial because remember, friends, Jesus is everything.

In science and math, outliers skew the results. That is precisely God's plan for us and this world. Outliers become part of God's Kingdom work, causing change in our communities and in our world.

> Do not be conformed to this world, but be transformed by the renewal of your mind, that by testing you may discern what is the will of God, what is good and acceptable and perfect (Romans 12:2, ESV).

The goal, we suppose, is that much like a magnet, Christian outliers draw others (including other believers), one at a time, away from the comfortable cluster and toward God, creating a new cluster—a life-giving family of brothers and sisters destined for Heaven where Jesus will say, "Well done."

> But you are a chosen race, a royal priesthood, a holy nation, a people for his own possession, that you may proclaim the excellencies of him who called you out of darkness into his marvelous light (1 Peter 2:9, ESV).

And yes, let's not forget that bonus outcome of living as a Christian outlier—the cherry on top, if you will—the promise of Heaven and to be richly rewarded for our faith, obedience, and perseverance, as heirs in His Kingdom.

Reflections & Questions
SEVEN

Our physical world is lived through our senses—what we can see, taste, hear, smell, and feel. When Cortney's world broke upon her husband's admissions, her vision narrowed and her peripheral world slipped out of focus. Her sense of sight left her. In its place, the sense of touch exploded. Cortney felt her heartbeat intensify, her cheeks flush, the texture of the pillow into which she had planted her face, and the give of the carpet as she later raced up the stairs. Which of your senses is on hyper-alert when you encounter struggle or heartbreak? Can you suddenly hear the proverbial pin drop? Can you taste the salt in your tears? Or is it your sense of sight or touch that's heightened?

If we are created three-dimensionally (1 Thessalonians 5:23), what do you think occupies the spirit "layer" in those who are not (yet) Christ-followers? Or, another way to ask it: What are some of the things we try to fill that God-sized hole with when we're not filled with the Holy Spirit? Does that work?

When have you had the opportunity to choose God over yourself? Whom did you choose? If you chose God over self, how did it play out? Do you think it was worth it? If you chose your own comfort, what happened? Would you do it differently if you could?

How do you feel about Christians being outliers? Do you like that term? Does it give you a sense of security, purpose, and/ or hope? Or does it leave you feeling isolated? Alone? Anxious? Explain.

TRULY TRUST GOD

Becky

I am sitting on a pew next to my mom at church. I must be four or five. The memory is faint, and I strain to recall it. I feel compelled to raise my hand. The entire congregation is praying. The pastor is standing on the stage leading the prayer. I bow my head and close my eyes—my hand still in the air. The prayer ends. We begin gathering our things to leave. The pastor from the stage comes down the steps and bounds over to me. I can't remember his voice or his words, but I *feel the weight of his man-sized hand pat me on the head to celebrate my giving my life to Jesus Christ. My childlike mind isn't sure if I raised my hand to accept Jesus or simply because other people were doing it too. But, my adult hindsight can see it was the Holy Spirit that compelled me to raise my hand that day in church.*

I have felt the presence of the Holy Spirit in me since I was that little girl with her hand raised. I thought it was my conscience during childhood telling me to obey my mom and dad. (I didn't always listen!) In my teens, I attended a youth group and learned more about God. I began to sense it was not just my conscience telling me to be honest or to be friends with the kids that don't fit in. It was the Holy Spirit that I received the day I raised my hand in church. I tried to both obey the Holy Spirit in me and ignore Him as I navigated my teen years. I chose the latter many times.

In my twenties, I could feel God asking me for more: more of myself and more trust in Him. I did the thing Christian women do to grow in God. I joined a women's Bible study. One night, we went around the table to share what our favorite book of the Bible was and why. I had been a Christian my entire life, but I could not think of my favorite book because I had never really read the Bible. I grew up going to church and believing in God, but I never developed a relationship with Him. The Bible study we were working on at the time was in the book of Job.

When it was my turn to share, I panicked, put on a fake smile, and said, "The book of Job is looking pretty good."

Soon after, Shad and I joined an in-home Bible study together. That was when we both really started to grow with God and develop personal relationships with Him. The time came when I wanted to have a baby, and I took it to God. It was the first major decision I considered with God's plan in mind instead of my own. He asked me to trust Him and be patient. Not long after, He gave us a son and then a daughter.

God asked Shad and I to trust Him when we moved across the state with two toddlers in tow. He used that experience to teach us about His Church and He gave us lifelong friends and Christian mentors. He made a new experience a great experience.

In 2012, I was diagnosed with skin cancer. I was scared and had to think about my own mortality while being a mom to three kids. He comforted me and healed my cancer with radiation. As God always came through for me, my trust in Him grew stronger.

After the cancer scare, God asked Shad and I to consider international adoption. We were nervous, but we said yes. We did all the paperwork and submitted it to Bulgaria. And then we patiently waited to be matched with a child, trusting His timing. We waited . . . and waited . . . and waited. After three years, we began to doubt. We wondered if God really did ask us to adopt.

We almost considered changing course. And then, we received the email with the little girl with the big, brown eyes.

Shad and I were in sync with each other and with God. We worked together like a well-oiled machine. When I was torn between being at the hospital with Rebeka and home with the big kids, Shad handed me a color-coded schedule with all the family members and friends that agreed to come and help. I no longer had to worry about being in two places at once. Our conversations and prayers were the strongest they have ever been. There was power in them. We felt no insecurity in sharing our thoughts and fears, no matter how raw they were. Shad understood me. I understood him. We both thought we understood God.

And then she died.

We celebrated Rebeka's life on what would have been her third birthday, one month after she died. We served cupcakes and even sang "Happy Birthday." It was a beautiful time with friends and family filled with brightly-colored balloons and flowers. Everyone wore their favorite party clothes and brought toy gifts to donate to Rebeka's hospital. As the party waned and we cleaned up, I began to feel tired. When we arrived home from the service and moved all the decorations and donations into the garage, Shad and I crashed. The adrenaline of the last five months disappeared, and the heaviness of grief took hold. We each retreated into our own way of grieving.

I was unable to focus on anything but sadness for months. Slowly, my mind made room for new thoughts and emotions. Doubt in God's plan. Asking *why*. Anger. I used to feel so confident that God's plan was good. What I came to realize was that all my life, I had trusted God's plan because it had seemed to always go the way I wanted it to. That realization was a hard pill to swallow. Perhaps you have had to choke down that same pill?

I don't like to doubt God. I already have so many insecurities about myself and others. Suddenly, my one constant security was gone. I didn't want to be, but I became angry with God. How could He trick us like that? He asked us to go after Rebeka. We were obedient. That means it should have turned out good, right? The way I wanted it to? How can God be good when the outcome was not? And then I would feel guilty for doubting His goodness. Romans 8:28 says:

> *And we know that in all things God works for the good of those who love him, who have been called according to his purpose.*

How can anything good come out of the death of my daughter? My anger was ugly and accusatory. I shook my fist at God and demanded answers. I fell on my face in despair and asked for relief from the sadness. Through the questions, anger, and sorrow, I sensed that child-like conscience, the Holy Spirit, deep in my soul. He has not let go of me since. And I have not let go of His hand. I long to see God's good plan in my Rebeka story because I know He has one.

To be an outlier for God, we must believe He is good even when our circumstances really suck. That's the difference between the cluster of dots and the one on the outskirts. *The space between the two is trust.*

I share my wrestling match with you, dear reader, because I am sure you have felt similarly in your life. I am not an expert, but rather a woman who tries her best to follow God's good plan even when it feels awful. The same way Cortney trusted God's good plan in the middle of her heartbreak. The best gift God has given me is the gift of truly trusting Him.

What does *truly trusting* God mean? It is easy to trust God when the outcome is pleasant and things turn out how I want. I continue to trust God because He continues to come through. Trusting God when life has fallen apart and He doesn't give you the happy ending you want . . . *that* is truly trusting God.

Like Cortney, I have made choices to get to this place of trust in my life:

- I have filled six journals in the last four years. I sit in my favorite chair most days and write my thoughts and feelings out as if I am talking to God. I read His Word, write it out, and meditate on it. I give everything to God because He is my Wonderful Counselor.

- When my mind gets dark, I put in my headphones and listen to worship music. There is no greater resetting of my thoughts than when I worship Jesus.
- This one is not always easy, but I have hard conversations with Shad. We both grieve in completely different ways. It is easy to misunderstand each other. The only way we can stay in sync is to be honest and open.
- On a sunny day, I go to Rebeka's grave and sit with her. The tangible act of cleaning her grave marker and placing flowers there is sacred. As her mom, not being able to take care of her feels empty. This is one way to fill that void.
- I make a choice every day to stay connected to God. I never let go of His hand.
- I chose to forgive God for not giving me the ending I wanted. I chose not to stay angry at Him.
- When life feels too hard, I pray for God's strength.

My family and I are still healing. Some of us enjoy talking about Rebeka, and for others it is difficult. We tell stories about her bossiness, and we laugh. All of us agree saying yes to her was the best choice we ever made. My kids are growing up and share lessons they learned from their baby sister: empathy, love, facing fear, and joy. Rebeka's life with us has even led one child down a path to a future career in healthcare. God has used the healing process to bring my family closer together and teach us to understand each other better. God has asked us to consider international adoption again. It feels even riskier this time, but we are choosing to trust Him and go down that path. We trust that He will be faithful to continue His story through the expansion of our family.

I hope you can see that life with God is a journey. No one does it perfectly, and our paths are unique. God has a different plan for each one of us. One thing that is constant is we have choices to make. My prayer is you will choose to say yes to God in the face of excitement, anticipation, doubt, and even fear. That you will say yes to being an outlier for God's good purpose and glory.

Reflections & Questions
EIGHT

Are you a Christian that hasn't developed a personal and intimate relationship with God? What is holding you back? What is one thing you can do each day to begin building a relationship with Him? If you are a Christian, how can you help someone else trust God when He asks them to do "crazy" things?

Have you ever doubted God? Do you struggle to trust Him because of that doubt? Do you think it is possible to *truly* trust God? We encourage you to pray for God to show you how to truly trust Him and His faithfulness to you.

NINE
GOD-CALLED CHOICES

Cortney

Today, my husband and I share an intimacy that was born from walking through trauma while grasping the hand of God. It's a marriage focused on His will, His timing, and His love for us. It's a marriage built on trust and the firm foundation of the Lord's promises and principals.

It's not a perfect marriage; it's not even the best marriage—though we think it's pretty fantastic. We flounder from time to time, occasionally feeling distant from one another and even from God. But it's a *good* marriage. A God-good one. And in that truth, we pray you find hope.

We pray you have hope even if your marriage story ended differently. Even if your health crisis continues. Even if your cross to bear is a lifelong struggle. In all things, God is present. He is holy, and He is good.

I wish there was a secret combination of character traits or detailed instructions I could provide, pointing other couples toward an intimate, God-good marriage. It would be terrific if a single self-help book existed, one outlining the steps to the perfect marriage, and miraculously, those steps worked for everyone. But there isn't. God created us all uniquely and blessed each of our unions with certain strengths, challenges, and giftings. No two marriages are the same, just as no two individuals are the same. Each marriage carries a special mission.

Here is what I've learned. (And it's the same lesson Becky shares, too):

> Your choices matter. Particularly the God-called ones.

We don't say this to overwhelm you or place too great a burden on your heart. We say this as a declaration of freedom.

We always have a choice. No matter what situation we find ourselves in, we can always, *always* seek out God. We can trust. We can utilize our third dimension, the indwelling Holy Spirit. We can respond with grace and in truth and love.

These are the choices I made that I believe put me on the path to my current position. It's a position—a space—characterized with purpose, joy, and beauty. (And I want the same for you.)

- Even as a perfectionist, striving for success and happiness, I learned to accept I have faults, carry sin, and need grace. I chose to accept Christ into my life, acknowledging my need for a Savior.

- I surrounded myself with other believers and read books from strong Christian leaders who were able to point me in the right direction, help me build upon my new faith, giving me the foundation and the hope I needed to pursue the full life of Christianity (the abundant life He promises).

- Even when I didn't quite understand what I was reading all of the time, I chose to dive deeply into the Word of God, trusting that if I got to know Him better, I could align myself with His thoughts, His plans, and His goals (the choice of less of me, more of Him).

- I chose to see God's hand in my life, never giving in to the temptations to avoid ridicule, doubt His goodness, or accept the misery caused when we wave off miracles and call them coincidences. I do not believe in coincidences.
- When tragedy struck, I listened. I didn't immediately react (despite desperately wanting to). I didn't give in to my swirling emotions or negative thoughts but listened to the Holy Spirit (my spiritual dimension).
- I chose to trust God, even when everything else inside me wanted to give up. I stood on the edge of a spiritual valley, choosing the mountain of faith over the hill of fear, humility over pride, and mercy over revenge.
- I chose to wrestle through all the layers of forgiveness required for complete healing (yes, it's a choice!).
- I chose to live as a rebel against worldly expectations, as an outlier for His Kingdom's cause, no matter the perceived (or real) personal cost.

And guess what? You can make these choices, too. It's not easy. The truth is, you cannot do it alone. It takes a strong support system of other Christ-minded people. If you don't have this kind of person or group of people in your life, ask God to provide them. He knows exactly who you need . . . and when.

I couldn't have reached these choices without friends, Christian leaders, or (believe it or not) my husband.

The choice to follow God is a choice to accept an invitation to live with and experience Greatness. We don't choose God initially; He chooses us. But we must decide to accept His invitation and then reaffirm that choice daily. Because each day that we open our eyes and take a breath is a day He has offered to us to live out a purposeful life, abundant and fruitful.

> You did not choose me, but I chose you and appointed you that you should go . . . (John 15:16).

What has He appointed you to do? Where has He appointed you to go? Is it illogical? Risky? Ridiculous? I kind of hope so. You see, I'm confident He will help you choose when to stand out from the crowd. It's a choice that will come at some point, if it hasn't already. It's best to decide now how you're going to respond to His call.

Finally, in math, research, and science, the best way to detect outliers is to graph the data. Those dots pop into view, much like the North Star on a clear night. Some researchers detest outliers. They skew the results so that the mean is no longer representative of the collective. In essence, they pull the cluster group in a different direction.

But, isn't that God's plan? To draw His children to Him? To help us fulfill our God-given purposes for which He created us? *Shouldn't that be our goal too?*

> Jesus, undeterred, went right ahead and gave his charge: "God authorized and commanded me to commission you: Go out and train everyone you meet, far and near, in this way of life, marking them by baptism in the threefold name: Father, Son, and Holy Spirit. Then instruct them in the practice of all I have commanded you. I'll be with you as you do this, day after day after day, right up to the end of the age (Matthew 28:19–20, MSG).

Continued assessment is one of the best ways to understand how certain outlying points (individuals) influence others. In Christianity, this assessment comes in the form of questions from the cluster itself as its members watch you live out God's good purposes for your life. As you bear witness to God's faithfulness and goodness, stepping outside comfort and expectation to do something you couldn't do apart from a holy God.

"How did you . . . ?"

"Why would you . . . ?"

"What makes you so different?"

Think before you respond. Your answers are meant to change the world.

Reflections & Questions
NINE

Have you run from a God-called choice? Talk or write about it. Release the guilt and shame. Now, fix your eyes on the choices you have made in your life up to this point that have prepared you to make the next God-over-self choice. Make a list, as Cortney and Becky did, of ordered choices that have built up your faith over time.

What is one choice you can make today that will move the worldly cluster of people in your sphere of influence in the direction of God's Kingdom? [For the next forty days, ask that question every morning, listening for God's answer so that each day, you're choosing to live out God's good purposes.

CLOSING PRAYERS

Becky

Dear God,

After Rebeka died, I thought I had You all figured out. I could see so clearly how You used her to change my heart and show me how to love more completely. I believed Rebeka was healed and in a perfectly healthy body. She was no longer in pain. It all made sense.

As the adrenaline of the journey wore off, I began to feel

things other than just the weight of grief. My sadness began to feel more like anger and doubt. I started to question all of it. To question *You*. I wondered if I would ever trust You again, and it scared me. You asked me to go after Rebeka, and she died. How could I trust You when You asked me to do anything else ever again?

You have been so faithful to allow me to ask these questions. You have been so patient and gentle. I stomp my foot and ask why, and You comfort me. You have shown me that I can simultaneously doubt You and have faith in You. I can feel angry and completely lost while feeling safely wrapped in your loving embrace. Some days, I have to strain to feel You close, but I always find You. You have never left my side. I thank You for that.

My prayer is that anyone who is afraid to trust You will surrender to Your will. That they will set aside fear and trade it for a holy confidence in Your plan. And I pray that anyone who feels doubt in You will allow You to make them brave enough to face that doubt so they can see that on the other side, is a closer relationship with You.

Amen.

Cortney

Heavenly Father,

As the wife of an addict, I discovered I had offered all of my devotion to a single person, and it wasn't Jesus. I had propped my husband up on a pedestal, thinking he could do no wrong. The weight of responsibility I put on his shoulders only inflamed the dysfunction and prevented him from seeking help for this addiction sooner.

I've learned how to seek out You first, and each time, You have *then* given me permission to turn to him, the man you anointed to be my husband. You've taught me the correct order of things.

As the wife of a recovering addict, I have also learned grace beyond measure. I've learned that Your way, Your truth, and Your Light are unparalleled. I've learned choosing to be a Christian outlier is worth it. Sometimes, I still can't believe my husband and I are still married. It's hard to understand how a seemingly happy marriage turned into a *phenomenal* marriage because of this crisis. When I seek out the reason, the only answer I've found is *You.*

Yet . . . in my daily comings and goings, I admit that I often fail to keep You at the center of my world. Sometimes, it's because I seek my own glory, chasing after idols I believe will fulfill my dreams. Idols such as praise, success, even happiness. Other times, the distractions of this world undermine my ability to focus on Jesus. Regardless of the reason, I forget You at best and ignore You at worst.

Sometimes, I forget how You met me on that comforter years ago, when my life had been torn apart, and I had nowhere to turn. I forget how You covered me with your grace, Your very wings, as I lay in child's pose on the closet floor day after day as You worked out Your goodness. I forget how You restored the things no one deemed restorable and You guided me to forgive the unforgivable.

But when I do remember, I am filled with both godly sorrow and wonder. Sorrow that I continue to strive for my own goals through my God-given competence and wonder at the how and why You give me chance after chance to get it right. Faith and intimacy with You are daily choices, and there are days, I admit, I turn away from You in silence or busyness.

I'm grateful You are a God who forgives, who hears our cries of desperation, who calls us to a purpose bigger than ourselves, and who gifts us with grace and mercy beyond measure.

My prayer is that those who are afraid of Your plans, who run from Your call, or who fail to trust You implicitly will rise above the doubt and fear—myself included. I pray their desire to glorify You is bigger than the comfort they currently experience. I pray they choose to become outliers for Christ, people willing to trust that Your love for them is fierce, and You are as good as You say you are.

I pray we are people, Your people, willing to choose You over popular opinion, cultural expectations, and even our own learned behaviors—certainly that we are sons and daughters who never twist Your Word to suit our perceived needs or selfish desires.

I pray those reading this choose You more often than I do.
In Jesus's name, amen.

Reflections & Questions
TEN

In Becky's prayer, she admits to feeling anger and doubt toward God. Have you ever felt that way toward God? Would you consider taking those feelings to God and allowing Him to guide you through to healing? Is it possible to need to forgive God when things don't go the way you hoped?

In Cortney's prayer to God, she admits how her shortcomings and the world around us can be distractions from keeping our eyes on Jesus. What idols, sin, or temptations hold you back from seeking out God on a daily basis?

Christ died for us all—not only for those who commit what we would label the biggest sins of all. Take a few minutes to pray a prayer of repentance, uncovering the godly sorrow that triggers true change.

Thank you for joining us on this journey. We hope you'll make the outlier's choice when God calls you to step away from what's expected to follow His good plan.

ABOUT THE AUTHORS

Becky Huber

Becky is a closet writer who prefers to keep it that way. She enjoys spending her quiet time journaling her thoughts and feelings to God. As she prepared to adopt internationally, God told her she would be telling her story to many. With a lot of trepidation, she is writing a memoir detailing her story of adop-  tion, childhood cancer, and walking through the grief of the loss of a child. She has shared her story on *Our Terminal* and *Lost Sparrows* Facebook and Instagram pages. Becky lives in the Pacific Northwest in Vancouver, Washington. Most days, you can find her talking cars with her teenage son, sipping iced coffee with her teenage daughter, building Legos with her younger daughter, or trying to find a quiet place to catch up with her husband, Shad.

Cortney Donelson

Cortney is a God-wrestling, humming-bird-watching, marriage lover. She is the owner and principal writer at vocem LLC, as well as co-founder and editor of *GirlStory* Magazine. While she has ghost-written several books, there is one other she can call her own, a memoir titled *Clay Jar Cracked: When We're Broken But Not Shattered,* which describes her marriage crisis and the subsequent journey to redemption in vivid detail. She is a speaker and Bible study facilitator and has appeared as a guest on *The 700 Club* and *Bloom Today* talk show. As the associate publisher of Fiction for Morgan James Publishing, she enjoys reviewing and recommending books for publishing. She calls Charlotte, North Carolina home where she enjoys paddle boarding, hiking, and escaping to the beach with her husband, Marc, their two kids, and a golden retriever named Lucas, who doesn't like to retrieve. You can find her at www.yourvocem.com.

A free ebook edition is available with the purchase of this book.

To claim your free ebook edition:

1. Visit MorganJamesBOGO.com
2. Sign your name CLEARLY in the space
3. Complete the form and submit a photo of the entire copyright page
4. You or your friend can download the ebook to your preferred device

A **FREE** ebook edition is available for you or a friend with the purchase of this print book.

CLEARLY SIGN YOUR NAME ABOVE

Instructions to claim your free ebook edition:
1. Visit MorganJamesBOGO.com
2. Sign your name CLEARLY in the space above
3. Complete the form and submit a photo of this entire page
4. You or your friend can download the ebook to your preferred device

Print & Digital Together Forever.

Snap a photo

Free ebook

Read anywhere

Printed in the USA
CPSIA information can be obtained
at www.ICGtesting.com
JSHW080001150824
68134JS00021B/2219